DECADES OF THE 20th AND 21st CENTURIES

The 1950s

Stephen Feinstein

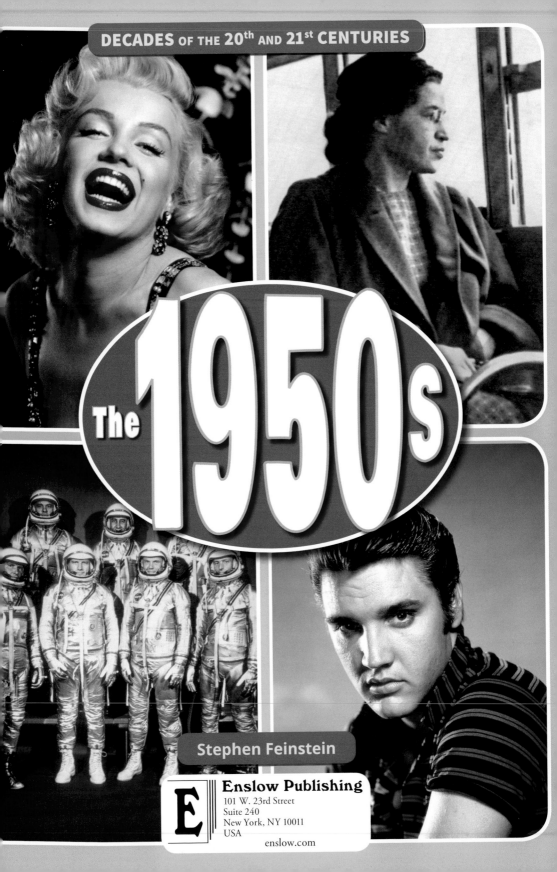

Enslow Publishing
101 W. 23rd Street
Suite 240
New York, NY 10011
USA

enslow.com

DECADES OF THE 20TH AND 21ST CENTURIES

The 1950s

Stephen Feinstein

Published in 2016 by Enslow Publishing, LLC.
101 W. 23rd Street, Suite 240, New York, NY 10011

Library of Congress Cataloging-in-Publication Data
Feinstein, Stephen.
The 1950s / Stephen Feinstein.
    pages cm. — (Decades of the 20th and 21st centuries)
Includes bibliographical references and index.
Summary: "Discusses the decade 1950-1959 in the United States in terms of culture, art, science, and politics"— Provided by publisher.
Audience: Grade 9 to 12.
ISBN 978-0-7660-6930-5
1. United States—Civilization—1945- —Juvenile literature. 2. United States—Politics and government—1953-1961—Juvenile literature. 3. United States—Politics and government—1945-1953—Juvenile literature. 4. Nineteen fifties—Juvenile literature. I. Title.
E169.12.F4469 2015
973.918—dc23

                        2015010947

Printed in the United States of America

To Our Readers: We have done our best to make sure all Web sites in this book were active and appropriate when we went to press. However, the author and the publisher have no control over and assume no liability for the material available on those Web sites or on any Web sites they may link to. Any comments or suggestions can be sent by e-mail to customerservice@enslow.com.

Contents

Introduction

During the 1950s, Americans experienced a wave of prosperity. After the previous two decades, which had been marked by a world war and economic disaster, the 1950s seemed like a relief. Many Americans were able to build careers and raise their families comfortably. Jobs were plentiful. More Americans could realize the American dream—a home of their own—perhaps in one of the new suburbs springing up all over the country.

Americans had earned the right to enjoy their newfound affluence. World War II—that enormous conflict that ended in 1945—had changed the world forever. In the years that followed, while Europe and Asia struggled to rebuild, America emerged from the war stronger than ever. The United States helped its allies—and even its former enemies—to recover. America also grew into a superpower with the influence and resources to lead other nations.

There was another superpower in the 1950s: the Soviet Union. The United States and the Soviet Union had been allies during World War II, but their alliance did not last long. The two nations held vastly different beliefs. The Soviet Union was based on a political ideology called communism, which Soviet leaders wanted to spread around the world. Under communism, all people were supposed to work together for the common good. No single person owned property; instead, everyone shared it. To make communism function, the Soviet government forced its citizens to follow many restrictive rules that did not allow them to live freely.

This system clashed sharply with the American ideals of liberty and independence. The Soviet goal of spreading communism around the world worried many Americans. They feared that communist spies were living among them. Soon, a bitter rivalry grew between the United States and the Soviet Union. Each tried to gain an advantage over the other, and each sought out other countries to serve as allies. The superpowers also built huge armies in case of war. Yet both sides knew that a war between them would be extremely dangerous. America and the Soviet Union both possessed nuclear weapons that, if used, might wipe out all of humanity.

The two superpowers carefully avoided a direct conflict but found other ways to fight. Their struggle came to be known as the Cold War, and it would last more than four decades.

American and Soviet diplomats argued in the United Nations, which faced its first Cold War crisis in 1950. The Soviet Union ally North Korea invaded the US ally South Korea. United Nations troops from around the world went to Korea to stop them. The bloody Korean War would drag on for three years.

While American and other soldiers fought in Korea, changes were taking place in the United States. African Americans were demanding equal rights. Teens danced to a new music called rock 'n' roll. Men and women were getting married and having children at a high rate, which is a phenomenon known as the baby boom. These events would reshape American society. Trends that began in the 1950s still affect the nation today. This decade would go down in history as one of sharp contrasts and unique happenings.

Soldiers came home from World War II ready to begin their lives.

Pop Culture, Lifestyles, and Fashion

In contrast to the years of economic hardship during the Great Depression of the 1930s and the strict rationing of goods during the years of World War II, the 1950s were a time of consumerism.

A Nation of Consumers

A consumer-oriented lifestyle was developing among the rapidly growing middle class. All sorts of things were now available to Americans. Many people now had money to spend on television sets and household appliances, such as refrigerators, dishwashers, and washing machines. Americans by the millions also bought cars. And the ultimate goal of the American dream—home ownership—was now also within reach of a great many Americans.

To make it easier and more convenient for American consumers to spend their money, some businesses during the 1950s began offering credit cards. Diner's Club provided the first credit card. Diner's Club was formed by Frank X. McNamara, an attorney. One day in 1950, McNamara was embarrassed when he found himself short of cash after eating dinner in a restaurant. The Diner's Club credit card allowed club members to dine at twenty-seven New York City restaurants. Instead of having to carry cash around, Diner's Club members only

Frank X. McNamara founded the Diner's Club charge card.

had to show a Diner's Club credit card. American Express began issuing credit cards in 1958. More than 250,000 Americans eagerly signed up for the credit cards during one three-month period. Bank of America then jumped on the bandwagon by issuing BankAmericards, which later became Visa. Today's MasterCard grew out of credit cards issued by banks in Chicago and California.

With postwar prosperity came 1950s consumerism. Both jobs and goods were plentiful, and Americans enjoyed their newfound purchasing power.

Cars Become More Popular

In a television commercial, Dinah Shore sang, "See the USA in your Chevrolet." Americans set out to do just that. General Motors' Chevrolet was one of the most popular cars during the 1950s. By the end of the decade, there were no fewer than forty-six different Chevrolet models available. Automobile manufacturers sent a loud and clear message to Americans: Cars are fun, and it is fun to drive! Americans heard the message and bought more cars than in any previous period. Especially popular were big long cars with tail fins. By 1952, there were more than fifty-two million cars on the roads across America.

Hitting the Highways

With all the cars on the road, traffic congestion was becoming a problem. Many of the nation's roads were in poor condition and were too narrow for easy travel. So in 1956, Congress passed the National Defense Highway Act, proposed by President Dwight D. Eisenhower. As a young army officer, Eisenhower had driven across the country and found the trip to be slow and difficult. He was concerned that armed forces would not be able to move around the country with speed if the situation arose. The president wanted to construct a network of efficient highways similar to Germany's autobahn.

The law approved the construction of a nationwide system of interstate freeways. The planned 42,500 miles of divided highway would eventually link every major city in the country. The thirty-five-year project was the world's largest highway network. America's interstate highway system is named in Eisenhower's honor. It forever changed the way Americans lived and traveled.

Comfortable Conformity

In the 1950s, those who had achieved the ultimate goal of the American dream were living in the best of all possible worlds—the

WEST

INTERSTATE
MINNESOTA
90

The interstate highway system improved travel considerably.

Disneyland

On July 17, 1955, an attraction opened that would become synonymous with America around the world. Disneyland, a theme park built by famed animator Walt Disney, opened with twenty attractions. The park became a vacation destination for families from California and eventually from around the country. 1950s children wore their "ears" almost religiously. Disneyland's magic was so powerful that even Soviet leader Nikita Krushchev wanted to visit the park on a scheduled trip to America. That request was denied.

   A sister site was built in Florida in 1971. Both parks have expanded considerably. The appeal of Disney has spread around the world. Paris, Hong Kong, Tokyo, and Shanghai now boast their own Disney parks.

American suburbs. At least, that is how it must have seemed to those who had yet to attain this goal. Suburban, middle-class American family life was glowingly portrayed each night on television as the epitome of easy living. The new American suburban lifestyle was characterized by conformity in external appearances, as well as in personal goals, opinions, and values. Not only did the streets and houses look the same, but so did the styles of clothing.

The typical suburban employee of a big corporation, who came to be called an organization man, commuted to work in the city. He wore a gray flannel suit or some equally conservative uniform to work. He kept his hair short. He usually wore a narrow-brimmed hat while traveling to and from work. The organization man's job was important to him whether he liked his work or not. He liked the suburban lifestyle it let him lead.

Rise of the Beat Generation

Some suburbanites eventually rejected what they considered the hollow values of the suburbs and the corporate world. Others were also turned off by the growing conformity they believed would stifle creativity in American life. Known as beatniks, these people—among them writer Jack Kerouac and poet Allen Ginsberg—rejected the culture of materialism and the conformity of organization men. They valued experience more than things and spontaneity more than routine. They challenged commonly held notions about how people should live, work, and play. Jack Kerouac set out on the road and crisscrossed America many times, even traveling through Mexico, in search of adventure and freedom. His 1957 novel, *On the Road*, is a fictional account of his experiences.

The beat lifestyle typically involved sexual freedom and the use of drugs, such as marijuana and alcohol. The beatniks could be seen hanging out in coffeehouses. They listened to jazz music and beat

Jack Kerouac was the poster boy for the beat generation.

poetry. Of course, not one of them would be wearing gray flannel or any other kind of suit. Many of the men, however, wore a different uniform: black turtleneck sweaters, blue jeans, sandals, and goatees. Beatnik women typically wore black leotards, short skirts, and long straight hair. Apparently, even those who rejected corporate ideas were not immune to conformity of some sort.

Women's Roles

Throughout the 1950s, women were often portrayed in magazines and advertisements as domestic servants whose main duty was catering to the needs of their husbands and children. According to *Life* magazine, a "truly feminine" woman's proper place was in the home, especially the kitchen.

In real life, however, more women were beginning to work outside the home in the 1950s. They had little time to prepare elaborate meals. By 1956, 32 percent of all women were part of the American labor force. Unfortunately, most women had to work at low-paying clerical, assembly line, or service jobs. Only a small number of women held management positions or practiced a profession. When women went into the kitchen after a hard day's work, they were likely to heat up frozen TV dinners for their families.

Although women's roles were changing, the most popular fashions of the 1950s emphasized women's femininity and sexuality. By 1950, Christian Dior's New Look had become the height of fashion. Dior's clothing enhanced a woman's natural curves and created the classic hourglass figure—skintight tailoring around the bosom, a narrow waist, and a full skirt that often flared out. Stiletto heels were popular, and many women did not feel completely dressed until they had painted their lips bright red. The well-dressed woman often wore a hat in public. Career women, dressed in suits, always wore gloves.

Baby Boomers

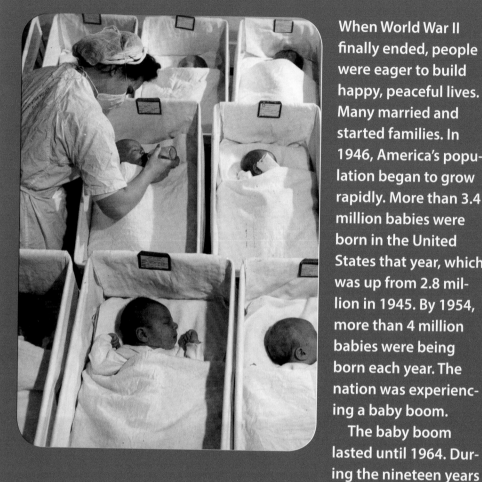

When World War II finally ended, people were eager to build happy, peaceful lives. Many married and started families. In 1946, America's population began to grow rapidly. More than 3.4 million babies were born in the United States that year, which was up from 2.8 million in 1945. By 1954, more than 4 million babies were being born each year. The nation was experiencing a baby boom.

The baby boom lasted until 1964. During the nineteen years of the baby boom, more than 76 million babies were born. Society scrambled to keep up with their needs. For example, new schools had to be built quickly for the growing number of students.

When the boomers grew up, they too began having children. This created a second smaller baby boom. Throughout their lives, the baby boomers have shaped American culture because of their large numbers.

Women favored feminine silhouettes, pearls, gloves, and a red lip.

Air Raids and Bomb Shelters

There was more going on in the 1950s than interesting fashions. In September 1949, Americans learned that their Cold War adversary, the Soviet Union, had built an atomic bomb. America was no longer the only nation with nuclear weapons. To Americans, the world had suddenly become much more dangerous. Soon, air-raid drills were being conducted across the country. When the siren sounded, people were to go to the nearest air-raid shelter and stay there until they heard the all-clear siren.

Even schoolchildren participated in air-raid drills. At the sound of the siren, teachers shouted, "Take cover!" The children would immediately follow the duck-and-cover routine they had been taught. They would get under their desks and put their head between their knees with their hands over their head. They were warned not to look at the window because they would be blinded by the flash of the nuclear explosion.

Although Americans were terrified of what could happen to them in a nuclear war, it is doubtful that many took the civil defense drills seriously. People were well aware of the incredible destruction that resulted from an atomic bomb. So when people were told to stay indoors or to avoid looking at the window, they had good reason to wonder how these measures could save them.

Still, there were many who believed they could survive a nuclear attack if they had access to a bomb shelter. Some Americans bought their own family shelters, which were installed in their backyards. Those who bought fallout shelters believed they were preventing the American dream from turning into the American nightmare.

Schoolchildren were trained to take cover during air raid drills.

It became popular to see how many people could fit in a telephone booth.

Crazy Fads

Americans in the 1950s were caught up in many popular fads. Perhaps to take their minds off the looming threats to America's security, people were enthusiastic about whatever seemed to be fun. College students could be seen stuffing themselves into telephone booths and cars, as if conducting serious research into the number of people that could fit into a small space. Some people stared in fascination as wire coils called Slinkies walked down flights of stairs. Some played with globs of moldable silicone called Silly Putty. Others tossed Frisbees.

Perhaps the most popular fad of the decade was the hula hoop, first introduced in 1958 by Arthur Melin and Richard Knerr of Wham-O Manufacturing. By 1959, millions of young Americans were swinging hula hoops around their hips, and soon, hula hoop contests were being held all around the country.

Entertainment and the Arts

The affluence of the 1950s and the baby boom created a growing entertainment industry. Suddenly, Americans had more time and money to devote to television and movies. Popular icons emerged that continue to fascinate us even today.

Teen Angst

In 1955, *Rebel Without a Cause* became a big hit with American teenagers. They identified with the film's young star, James Dean, who blamed his parents for his state of confusion and anguish. Many teens in the 1950s, especially those growing up in suburbs, were bored by the blandness of their surroundings. They were confused by society's standards and expectations for them and resentful of adults' lack of understanding.

Fictional characters showing the concerns of 1950s teenagers appeared in literature, as well as in film. Teen readers found their spokesman in Holden Caulfield, the teenage hero of J. D. Salinger's novel *The Catcher in the Rye* (1951). Holden Caulfield shared their frustration with the hypocrisy of adult values.

Teens identified with James Dean's angst in Rebel Without a Cause.

Marlon Brando's new style of realistic acting inspired young people.

In 1954, the young actor Marlon Brando starred in *The Wild One*. In the film, he played the leader of a motorcycle gang. The movie inspired young people who identified with the bikers' desire to test the limits of society's tolerance for delinquent behavior. While young people related to the film's heroes, older Americans were becoming concerned with problems of juvenile delinquency and gang-related crime. Movies, such as *The Blackboard Jungle* (1955), pointed out the ugly behavior of unruly youth in New York City's schools.

Some movies of the 1950s depicted social issues. *The Blackboard Jungle* dealt with teen violence.

The Appeal of Science Fiction

As if Americans in the 1950s did not have enough to worry about with nuclear weapons, there was something new to fear—an invasion from outer space! Hollywood produced a number of science fiction films dealing with extraterrestrial visitors, such as *War of the Worlds* (1953) and *Invasion of the Body Snatchers* (1956). Many people were either thrilled or horrified by the antics of space creatures on the big screen. Others reported seeing flying saucers—strange lights in the night skies over America. Nobody could prove whether the UFOs—unidentified flying objects, as the lights came to be called—were real and perhaps visitors from another planet or just a figment of people's imaginations.

Advances in Technology at the Movies

Movie producers in the 1950s were afraid that Americans would be so fascinated by television and all the entertainment they could enjoy in their own living rooms that they would forget to go to the movies. So the movie industry came up with new ideas to attract an audience. They began to use a wide-screen process, known as CinemaScope, while often presenting biblical spectacles with casts of thousands, such as *The Ten Commandments* (1956) and *Ben-Hur* (1959).

Producers also made movies that gave the illusion of three dimensions. In 3-D horror films, such as *House of Wax* (1953), *It Came from Outer Space* (1953), and *Creature from the Black Lagoon* (1954), the illusion of depth was so vivid that moviegoers would often duck as things seemed to leap off the screen and into their laps. There was only one catch—in order to experience the third dimension, moviegoers had to wear special glasses. Many people found these glasses annoying. Some even reported getting headaches.

Science Fiction's Golden Age

In the 1950s, many great science fiction authors were writing their best stories. One of the genre's most notable, Isaac Asimov, was both a writer and a respected scientist. In 1950, he wrote *I, Robot*. The book told of a future in which humans and robots work together. During his long career, the Russian-born Asimov wrote more than four hundred books.

Ray Bradbury imagined a more troubling future. His stories were often about the dangers of technology. His novel *Fahrenheit 451* was published in 1953. In the chilling tale, people are discouraged from thinking. Television rules society, and books are illegal. If found, they are promptly burned. *Fahrenheit 451* is still known today as a classic work of science fiction.

Arthur C. Clarke was a British author who served in the Royal Air Force during World War II. Afterward, he studied the sciences in college. Clarke began writing science fiction books in the 1950s. His most famous novel, *2001: A Space Odyssey*, which was adapted into an Academy Award-winning film, was published in 1968.

A Generation of Little Cowboys

Along with sitcoms and variety shows, Westerns were among the most popular television shows of the 1950s. Galloping across the screen were popular cowboys, such as Hopalong Cassidy, the Lone Ranger, the Cisco Kid, Roy Rogers, and Gene Autry.

Westerns especially appealed to children, who spent long hours in front of the television, riding along with their favorite heroes. Before long, millions of young children were prowling the streets of America, wearing big cowboy hats, and firing their toy cap guns at each other in mock gunfights. By the mid-1950s, more sophisticated Westerns, such as *Gunsmoke* and *Have Gun Will Travel,* were being made. These shows became popular mainly with adult audiences.

Tuning In to Television

Television became a part of American life in the 1950s. Before then, radio was the most popular form of entertainment. The major radio networks were NBC, CBS, and ABC. In the late 1940s, these networks made the move to television. Sales of TV sets soared.

Early television was much different from the TV we know today. There were very few channels. Color TV was not yet available, so all shows were in black and white. There was no way to record or save programs in the home.

Still, television quickly became a main source of family entertainment. For the first time, people could watch moving images from the comfort of home. Some of America's most popular radio programs went on to become TV shows, but there were also some original shows. In 1950, CBS debuted a game show called *What's My Line?* that ran for decades. A year later came the comedy *I Love Lucy*, starring Lucille Ball, that remains one of the most beloved shows in TV history.

Marilyn Monroe

The sexual revolution that would erupt in America in the 1960s was starting to simmer in the 1950s. Perhaps the one person who best symbolized Americans' fantasies and notions about sexuality in the 1950s was Marilyn Monroe. Born Norma Jean Mortenson in 1926, Monroe grew up to become a screen sensation during the 1950s. She starred in such films as *Gentlemen Prefer Blondes* (1953), *How to Marry a Millionaire* (1953), and *Some Like It Hot* (1959). Marilyn Monroe did indeed have a beautiful face and body, but she was also a fine actress and singer. She put her comedic skills to good use by satirizing the Hollywood sex goddess role that made her famous.

Marilyn Monroe was the beauty ideal of the 1950s.

The King

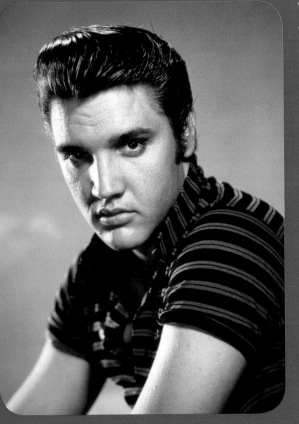

The first rock 'n' roll hit was "Rock Around the Clock," performed by Bill Haley and the Comets in 1955. Teens enjoyed the song's snappy melody. Before long, there were many famous rock 'n' roll artists. Chuck Berry scored a hit with "Johnny B. Goode" in 1958; Buddy Holly sang "Peggy Sue" in 1957; and Little Richard's "Good Golly Miss Molly," another rock 'n' roll classic, was released in 1958.

Elvis Presley was the biggest rock 'n' roll star to emerge in the 1950s. Born in Mississippi in 1935, Presley taught himself to play the guitar. At the age of twenty-two, he already had five number one songs, including "Hound Dog" and "Don't Be Cruel." Elvis would go on to notch thirty number one hits in his career. He also starred in movies. Elvis Presley became one of the most famous entertainers in the world. Although he died in 1977, he is still considered one of America's most important popular icons today. Rock 'n' roll fans still remember Elvis Presley fondly as the King.

Rock 'n' Roll Arrives

In his hit rock 'n' roll song "Roll Over Beethoven," singer Chuck Berry told Beethoven, who symbolized classical music, to "roll over." He might just as well have advised every other older musical style to roll over and get out of the way because rock 'n' roll was here to stay. Due to its almost instant popularity among America's teens, rock 'n' roll swept aside all other forms of music.

Rock 'n' roll did not just appear overnight. It was based on a combination of black blues and R&B (rhythm and blues) and white blues, or hillbilly music. What these kinds of music had in common was their soulful expression of raw emotion. Rock 'n' roll was a huge success because it had a winning formula—simple melodies, basic chords, and a backbeat. It featured a new instrument known as the electric guitar. It was loud and sexy. There was nothing subtle about it. And rock 'n' roll was great to dance to, as seen on Dick Clark's television show *American Bandstand*. An added benefit of rock 'n' roll was that older Americans, including the parents of teenagers, hated it. When young Americans went crazy over rock 'n' roll, the older generation reacted with alarm in fear that the music was wildly sexual and would lead young people astray. So millions of American teens, especially those with a rebellious streak, became devoted fans of 1950s rock stars, such as Jerry Lee Lewis, Buddy Holly, Chuck Berry, Little Richard, and Fats Domino. The biggest rock 'n' roll sensation was Elvis Presley, who came to be called the King of rock 'n' roll.

Rock 'n' roll was able to succeed in part because there were so many young people to enjoy it. A post–World War II baby boom led to such a high birthrate that by 1958, one third of America's population was under the age of fifteen. This new generation of Americans would eventually create a new youth culture based on rock 'n' roll music.

Teenagers of the 1950s danced to the songs of Fats Domino.

Changes in Jazz

True jazz fans in the 1950s were not about to give up the music they loved. While rock 'n' roll got hotter, jazz became cool—real cool. In previous decades, jazz had been widely popular because people liked to dance to it. But by the 1950s, the most interesting and innovative jazz was not dance music, and the audience for it was much smaller. Fans enjoyed listening to the brilliant, intricate improvisations of musicians, such as Miles Davis, Theolonious Monk, Dizzy Gillespie, Sonny Rollins, John Coltrane, and McCoy Tyner. The music had become serious, and it required concentration on the part of listeners. Audiences would sit quietly in rapt attention while the cool sounds of the Modern Jazz Quartet wafted over them.

Trumpeter and bandleader Miles Davis took jazz in new directions. Davis' 1959 album *Kind of Blue* is widely considered a jazz masterpiece and the best selling jazz album of all time.

The Modern Jazz Quartet combined classical music, jazz, and bop.

A museum curator examines a 1950 Jackson Pollock painting.

Art Goes Abstract

What if an artist set out to create art specifically to outrage and shock people? And what if the intended audience not only refused to be offended but took an interest in the new kind of art? This is what happened in the art world during the 1950s.

Painters who, like the beatniks, rejected conformity and materialism were determined to rebel against limits on how they could paint. The first step in eliminating boundaries was to do away with the subject—there would be no recognizable image. Paintings, which tended to be huge, were abstract, and artists such as Jackson Pollock became known as abstract expressionists. In a sense, abstract expressionist paintings were often about the act of painting itself. Pollock devised a way to drip paint onto huge canvases stretched out on the floor. Others attacked the canvas, lunging with a knife or trowel. Artists such as these were called Action Painters. Art lovers were mostly baffled by the displays of blobs, drips, and scribbles at first. But gradually, the public came to accept and value the paintings of the would-be rebels. Within a few years, abstract expressionist paintings were not only hanging in art galleries and museums but could also be seen decorating the walls of corporate offices.

Jackie Robinson's
Dodgers finally won the
World Series in 1955.

Sports

Americans' love of sports continued to grow in the 1950s. Baseball became even more popular. Jackie Robinson had diversified baseball, and in 1950 Althea Gibson would do the same for tennis.

Focus on the Dodgers

Brooklyn Dodger fans were certainly among the most loyal and devoted fans in the history of baseball. Most likely, the perception of the Dodgers as a perpetual underdog helped stir up the passion of the fans, who affectionately referred to their favorite team as Dem Bums in the local Brooklyn accent. Time and time again, the Brooklyn Dodgers would come close to winning the World Series. And each time they would lose. The Dodgers faced their rivals, the New York Yankees, in the World Series in 1941, 1947, 1949, 1952, and 1953. Each time, the Dodgers lost even though they had exceptionally fine ball players, such as Jackie Robinson, Gil Hodges, Roy Campanella, and Johnny Podres. "Wait till next year" became the theme song of the Brooklyn Dodgers.

But then in 1955 Dem Bums finally defeated the New York Yankees in the World Series. The Brooklyn Dodgers were bums no longer. Unfortunately, the joy was short lived. In the 1956 World Series, the

Roy Campanella followed Jackie Robinson into the Major Leagues.

The Shot Heard 'Round the World

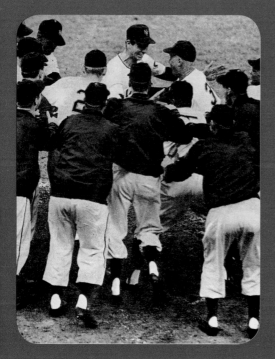

The 1951 National League pennant race came down to two New York teams: the Brooklyn Dodgers and the New York Giants. In the ninth inning of the final game of the playoff, Giants outfielder Bobby Thomson hit a three-run homer to turn what looked like certain defeat into victory for his team. Adding to the excitement was the fact that this was baseball's first nationally-televised game.

The home run was known as the shot heard 'round the world because millions of baseball fans in New York and across the country were able to watch the Giants' saved-from-defeat victory. In addition, the game aired on Armed Forces Radio so the servicemen stationed in Korea could listen to a slice of home.

The Giants lost to another New York team, the Yankees, in the World Series that year. But Thomson's home run is still remembered as one of the great sporting moments of the decade.

Bobby Thomson's home run was called the shot heard 'round the world.

Dick Button

In 1952, American figure skater Dick Button competed in his second Olympic Games. At the 1948 games in St. Moritz, Switzerland, he became the first skater to land a double-axel jump. This feat helped him win a gold medal. He repeated this accomplishment by landing a triple loop, which was the first triple jump ever completed during a competition, in the 1952 games in Oslo, Norway.

Button is regarded as one of the sport's best. In addition to his two Olympic golds, he is also a five-time World Champion. Button also holds a law degree and is an actor and television analyst.

Dodgers lost to the New York Yankees once again. Then in 1958, the Brooklyn Dodgers moved away and became the Los Angeles Dodgers. Some fans never forgave Dem Bums for leaving Brooklyn.

Boxing's Champ

Considered one of the hardest punchers in boxing history, Rocky Marciano held the world heavyweight boxing championship title from 1952 to 1956. Born in Massachusetts as Rocco Marchegiano, Marciano won his heavyweight title in September 1952 by defeating Jersey Joe Walcott. Marciano successfully defended his heavyweight title six times. He retired undefeated in 1956 having won all of his forty-nine professional fights.

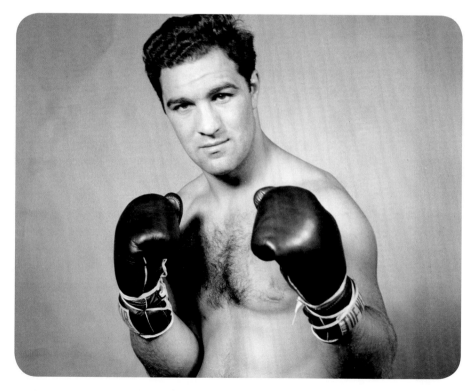

Rocky Marciano never lost or tied a boxing match during his entire four-year reign as heavyweight champion.

A Golfer Is Athlete of the Year

In 1953, the Associated Press named golfer Ben Hogan the male athlete of the year. The honor was well earned. Throughout his career, Hogan won more than sixty tournaments. He won the United States Open four times, the Masters twice, the Professional Golfers' Association (PGA) twice, and the British Open once. One of those tournament wins showed Hogan's tremendous ability to overcome obstacles. In 1949, Hogan was seriously injured in a car accident. Just seventeen months after the accident, still wearing bandages on his legs, Hogan not only played in the 1950 United States Open but also actually won the tournament!

During Ben Hogan's remarkable career, he had enormous influence on the sport's form.

Althea Gibson shattered records and stereotypes on the tennis court.

Althea Gibson Breaks Tennis's Race Barrier

For many years, tennis was predominantly a sport for white men, at least professionally. In the 1950s, Althea Gibson changed all that. One of the leading women's amateur players from 1950 to 1958, Gibson became the first well-known African American tennis player. Among other major victories, Gibson won two consecutive Wimbledon singles titles in 1957 and 1958, as well as the United States Open singles titles in both those years. She was the first African American player to win these important tournaments.

National and International Politics

Although the nation was settling into a postwar period of comfort and unprecedented prosperity, America in the 1950s saw plenty of turbulence. This included the fight for civil rights, paranoia about communism spreading to America's shores, and another military conflict.

McCarthyism

On February 9, 1950, Joseph McCarthy, a Republican senator from Wisconsin, announced that he had a list of 205 communists who worked in the State Department. If this sensational charge were true, America was in deep trouble. But in speeches over the next few days, McCarthy was vague when reporters asked for details. His list of 205 names shrank to 57, and then to just four names. It was also not clear whether the people named were actually communists, communist sympathizers, or people who somehow helped the cause of communism. But details did not seem to matter to the senator or to many of his listeners.

And so began McCarthy's four-year campaign of accusations and threats. McCarthy had shrewdly concluded that playing on Americans' fears of communism was a good way to win political power. People from Hollywood, the media, politics, and other walks of life

McCarthy claimed there were communists in the State Department.

The Rosenbergs were executed for spying for the Soviets.

were brought before McCarthy's committee and questioned by McCarthy and his faithful assistants, Roy Cohn and G. David Schine.

Many people lost their jobs as a result of McCarthy's activities. Careers were destroyed, and lives were wrecked. McCarthy, in a short time, became one of the most powerful and feared men in America. Few of his fellow politicians were willing to speak against him. They knew that many Americans at the time were genuinely afraid of communism.

Americans stood by while McCarthy continued to harass people. But in the fall of 1953, McCarthy finally bit off more than he could chew. He went after the United States Army and claimed he would expose the communists lurking there.

The Army-McCarthy hearings in 1954 were televised daily to an audience of eighty million viewers. On television, Americans saw McCarthy's mean-spirited behavior. This was the beginning of the end for McCarthy. Public opinion turned against him. Later that year, the Senate condemned McCarthy for his behavior. McCarthy lost his influence. He died in May 1957 from complications due to alcoholism.

The Rosenbergs

When the Soviet Union exploded an atomic bomb in 1949, Americans were shocked. Americans had assumed that the Soviet Union was far behind the United States in science and technology. It seemed that the only way the Soviets could have built a bomb was by stealing secrets from the United States. And the United States government was determined to expose spies who gave away secrets and put a stop to nuclear espionage.

In 1950, the Federal Bureau of Investigation (FBI) arrested Julius and Ethel Rosenberg. They had been named as members of a spy ring plotting to pass atomic secrets to the Soviets. The couple claimed they were innocent and would give no further information. The

Just five years after World War II ended, America was back at war.

Rosenbergs had been active members of the communist party during the 1930s but dropped out in 1943, when their first son was born. Ethel's brother, David Greenglass, had confessed to being part of the spy ring. He claimed that he had handed over secret documents to the Rosenbergs.

On March 29, 1951, a jury convicted the Rosenbergs of espionage. On April 5, Judge Irving Kaufman sentenced them to die in the electric chair. According to Kaufman, the Rosenbergs' crime was "worse than murder." Recent evidence shows that Julius Rosenberg was indeed guilty of spying. His wife was not, although she knew of her husband's activities.

The Rosenberg case divided America. Many Americans at the time felt that the Rosenbergs were innocent or that their sentence was too harsh. But many others believed the Rosenbergs had received a fair trial. In any case, the government was determined to make an example of them. On June 19, 1953, the Rosenbergs died in the electric chair.

Fighting Erupts in Korea

"We are going to fight!" said President Harry Truman to his daughter, Margaret, on June 25, 1950, upon learning that the communist North Korean Army had just invaded South Korea. Two days later, Truman, with the approval of the United Nations (UN) Security Council, ordered American military forces to help defend the South Koreans against the communists. America was at war again just five years after the end of World War II.

By 1950, it seemed to the United States that the communist Soviet Union and China were bent on world domination. The "free world"—the United States and its allies—would have to preserve its democratic way of life. When World War II ended in 1945, Korea, which had been occupied by the Japanese, was divided by an agreement between the United States and the Soviet Union. North Korea became a communist nation under dictator Kim Il Sung. South Korea was ruled by anticommunist dictator Syngman Rhee.

By 1950, the leaders of North and South Korea began boasting that they would unify all of Korea under their own rule. When the Soviet-supported North Korean Army finally invaded the South, the Cold War reached a boiling point. The North Koreans refused to withdraw. So the UN authorized forces, mainly American troops, to push them back.

Once the North Koreans began their invasion, they quickly captured Seoul, the South Korean capital, and pushed deep into the southern part of the country. The situation looked bleak. Then, American General Douglas MacArthur, in charge of the UN forces, devised a brilliant but risky strategy. On September 15, 1950, his troops surprised the North Koreans at Inchon, one hundred fifty miles behind enemy lines. The North Korean Army was forced to retreat. But many more battles lay ahead.

Truman Fires MacArthur

The war should have ended once the North Koreans left the South. After all, that had been the goal of the United States and United Nations intervention. But now President Truman, with the encouragement of General MacArthur, saw an opportunity to invade the North and unite both Koreas under the rule of the South. So the goal was revised.

With the approval of the United Nations, MacArthur's forces pushed northward. MacArthur assured President Truman that there was nothing to worry about—the Chinese would not attack. But suddenly, waves of Chinese troops swept across the border. During the bitterly cold winter of 1950 and 1951, the American forces suffered high casualties and were driven back to the 38th parallel.

In the end, Truman (right) had no choice but to relieve MacArthur of his duties.

POWs celebrate their release at the end of the Korean War.

MacArthur came up with another plan. He tried to convince Truman that they could win the war by bombing Chinese air bases in Manchuria. Truman wanted to win the war, but he also wanted to contain the fighting within Korea. He could not allow the conflict to grow into World War III given the fact that America and the Soviet Union both had atomic weapons and could destroy humankind. MacArthur would not take no for an answer. The Truman administration thought the most sensible plan was to forget about uniting the two Koreas and to seek a peace agreement that kept the country divided.

When MacArthur heard that Truman was planning to seek a cease-fire, he decided to challenge Truman's strategy. MacArthur spoke out in public arguing against the president's plans. President Truman, who was MacArthur's Commander in Chief, was furious. Although MacArthur was widely admired by Americans, his conduct was unacceptable. On April 11, 1951, Truman fired MacArthur. The soldier would not obey orders and was relieved of his command.

The Korean War Ends in a Draw

By the fall of 1952, the Korean War was already two years old. Tens of thousands of American soldiers had been killed or wounded in the war. Yet there seemed to be little progress on the battlefield. The UN troops and their communist foes had fought to a draw. Brutal fighting continued along the 38th parallel, the dividing line between North and South Korea. But neither side could score a major victory. A retired US General believed it was time to end the war.

Dwight D. Eisenhower was one of America's finest military leaders. During World War II, he helped defeat Nazi Germany. Afterward, he retired from the army. In 1952, Eisenhower decided to run for president. He told voters that, if elected, he would go to Korea. He wanted to find a way to stop the fighting. Americans were tired of the costly war. They elected Eisenhower to the presidency.

General Douglas MacArthur

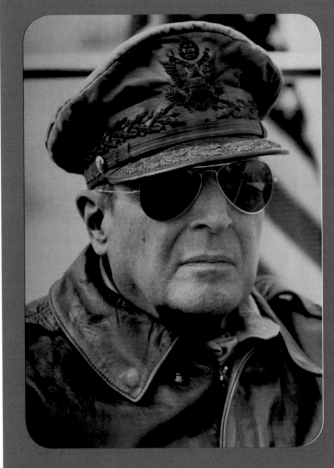

Douglas MacArthur was born in 1880. His father had been a Civil War hero. From the time he was a boy, Douglas wanted to be an army officer, too. He attended the US Military Academy at West Point, New York. Later, he led troops into battle during World War I. During World War II, MacArthur helped defeat Japan in the Pacific.

When the Korean War broke out, MacArthur was already seventy years old. Clearly, Korea would be the last war of his career. MacArthur desperately wanted to win it. Despite his defiance of President Truman, Douglas MacArthur remained very popular in the United States. He returned home to a hero's welcome.

Eisenhower kept his promise and traveled to Korea. He quickly saw that neither side could win. As president, he made it clear to North Korea and China that the United Nations wanted peace. He forcefully added that South Korea must never be attacked again. After months of talks, both sides agreed to a truce. The fighting in Korea finally came to an end in July 1953. There were no winners. Korea remained a land divided, as it had been before the war began. North and South Korea were in ruins, and their economies were destroyed. The war had claimed the lives of more than 2.5 million soldiers, including more than 35 thousand Americans.

Eisenhower's Presidency

As the Republican presidential candidate in the 1952 elections, Eisenhower ran on promises to end the war in Korea and to continue prosperity in America. Americans liked Ike, as Eisenhower came to be called.

Adlai Stevenson was the Democrats' candidate, but many Americans felt it was time for a change. There had not been a Republican president in office since Herbert Hoover in the early 1930s. So Americans proved how much they liked Ike by electing him.

Eisenhower proved to be a popular, although somewhat dull, president. His administration tended to favor the interests of big business. However, Eisenhower was involved in a large expansion of the Social Security system. He worked toward passage of the first civil rights act, in 1957, since Reconstruction ended in 1877. He also helped provide the first major federal funding for education and established the Department of Health, Education, and Welfare (HEW) as a Cabinet position in 1953. In 1956, voters still liked Ike. They reelected him to four more years in the White House.

At the end of Eisenhower's second four-year presidential term, he offered a warning to the American people. During his years as

General Dwight D. Eisenhower served two terms in the White House.

president, the old general had come to realize that a combination of powerful interests—the military establishment and the huge arms industry, which were supported by politicians, America's largest corporations, and defense research scholars—threatened to tie the nation's economic health to enormous defense budgets as far ahead as the eye could see. During his farewell to the nation just three days before leaving office, Eisenhower warned, "We must guard against the acquisition of unwarranted influence . . . by the military-industrial complex. The potential for the disastrous rise of misplaced power exists and will persist."

Mexican Labor

During World War II, many American farms, as well as certain industries such as railroads and trucking, relied on workers from Mexico to alleviate the labor shortage in the United States. In the past, the Mexicans had often been treated badly. Forced to labor under terrible working conditions, they had to live in housing that often consisted of nothing more than a chicken coop and often had nothing better to eat than leftover scraps of food. Unscrupulous employers sometimes did not even pay their Mexican workers.

In response to the labor shortage, the US government sought to encourage Mexicans to become temporary workers in this country. The government created the bracero program to enable American employers to recruit Mexicans. The word *bracero* (from *brazo*, or "arm" in Spanish) means someone who works with his arms, or a hired hand. The program was supposed to guarantee a minimum wage, encourage fair labor practices, and protect the health and well-being of the Mexican workers. But the abuse of Mexican workers continued.

Nevertheless, during the first bracero program, from 1942 to 1947, about 250,000 Mexicans were hired to work seasonally in the United States. During the second bracero program, from 1948 to 1964, more than 4.5 million Mexicans came to work in the United States. At the height of the program, in 1956, some 445,000 Mexicans worked in agriculture in the United States.

The Fight to Desegregate Education

For years since the end of the Civil War, African Americans, especially in the South, had to use separate facilities from white Americans—everything from separate restrooms to separate drinking fountains. Racist whites, who refused to grant blacks the equal rights they had won after the Civil War, referred to this system as separate but equal.

On May 17, 1954, the United States Supreme Court, in *Brown v. Board of Education of Topeka, Kansas*, finally ruled that separate facilities in regard to education were inherently unequal. At the time, 40 percent of American public schools were still segregated, or separated by race. The Supreme Court ordered them to be desegregated.

Even so, people's prejudices did not vanish overnight. When African American students tried to enter what had been all-white schools, they faced the bitter defiance of many Southern whites. For several years, there was very little progress in desegregating schools. Then, in 1957, African Americans in Little Rock, Arkansas, won a court order allowing nine African American students to enter Little Rock's Central High School. Arkansas Governor Orval Faubus, who opposed school integration, ordered the Arkansas National Guard to block the entrance to the school. For the next three weeks, photos of armed troops preventing the nine students from entering the school appeared in newspapers all across the country. On September 24, 1957, President Eisenhower sent a thousand army troops to Little Rock. On September 25, they made sure the African American students were allowed into the school.

These children were the plaintiffs in the Brown desegregation case.

Rosa Parks's arrest made her an icon of the Civil Rights movement.

Rosa Parks Refuses to Give Up Her Seat

Meanwhile, civil rights progress was being made in other areas. On December 1, 1955, Rosa Parks, an African American seamstress, was riding on a bus in Montgomery, Alabama. When the bus driver ordered her to give up her seat to a white man, she refused, thereby breaking the law. Parks was arrested, jailed, and fined ten dollars. The incident outraged Montgomery's African American community. Inspired by Rosa Parks's courageous act, Dr. Martin Luther King Jr. and other black civil rights leaders organized a peaceful boycott of Montgomery's bus system. The boycott lasted until December 20, 1956, when the United States Supreme Court ruled that Alabama's bus segregation laws were unconstitutional.

A Change in the Soviet Union

Joseph Stalin, the dictator who had ruled the Soviet Union since 1929, died in 1953. Although he had used secret police to terrorize the population and was responsible for the deaths of millions of Soviet citizens, many Soviets mourned his passing.

The new Soviet leader, Nikita Khrushchev, was determined to improve the lives of the Soviet people. After denouncing Stalin's misdeeds in a speech, Khrushchev made it clear that he intended to make reforms. He was in favor of easing the government's strict control of every aspect of life and the official censorship of the arts and media. Under Khrushchev, people began to enjoy a greater degree of freedom to express their views. But while a new day seemed to be dawning at home, the Soviet government maintained its tight grip over the other communist nations of Eastern Europe.

A Failed Revolution in Hungary

In October 1956, the Hungarian people rose up against the Soviet-backed government in their country. The rebellion became a mass movement, and Hungarian leader Imre Nagy (pronounced "Nahj") spoke out about breaking free of the Soviet Union's control. Some Hungarians took the occasion to seek revenge against Soviet secret police, who had killed many Hungarians in the past. Dozens of secret police were lynched.

Of course, the Soviet Union was not about to tolerate such a revolt. For several days, Hungarians celebrated their new freedom. The celebration did not last long, however. Soviet troops and tanks soon rolled into Hungary. Many Hungarian freedom fighters tried to resist the invaders. They appealed to the United States for help. But no help came because the Eisenhower administration did not want to risk a confrontation with the Soviet Union. In the next few days, more than twenty thousand Hungarian citizens were killed. Imre Nagy was arrested and executed by the Soviets.

Castro's Revolution

Since 1956, a revolution had been occurring only ninety miles away from Key West, Florida, in the Caribbean nation of Cuba. The rebels, under the command of Fidel Castro, were fighting to overthrow the brutal and corrupt dictatorship of Fulgencio Batista. Cuba was wealthy, but the distribution of wealth was very unequal. A small group of families controlled most of the wealth of the island. The rest of the population was very poor. Batista often jailed, tortured, and murdered his political opponents. Most Cubans hated him, and several groups wanted to overthrow him. Castro, on the other hand, attracted followers and even had admirers in the United States. By the late 1950s, Castro and his guerrilla fighters were gaining the upper hand against Batista's troops. Finally, in January 1959, Batista fled the island. Castro and his troops entered Havana in triumph.

Once in power, Castro instituted reforms to improve the lives of the poorest Cubans. In the process, he seized private companies and

Castro's regime hurt relations between the United States and Cuba.

Gaining Independence

At the end of World War II, there were still many colonies around the world. Parts of Asia and almost all of Africa were controlled by European countries, mainly Britain and France. But people in the colonies wished to be free from foreign rule, and during the 1950s, the drive for self-rule gathered steam.

Britain and France had fought together as Allied Forces during World War II with the purpose of defending freedom. It was only natural, then, that people in the British and French colonies would also demand their freedom. However, Britain and France did not grant independence to their colonies right away or without a struggle. An independence movement led by Mohandas Gandhi had finally helped convince Britain to let go of its largest and most important colony, India, in 1947. Other British colonies in Asia quickly followed. France tried to restore its control over southeast Asia after World War II but faced violent resistance. Cambodia won independence in 1953. Vietnamese fighters defeated the French the following year. In Africa, people in the colonies labored for freedom in a variety of ways. In some places there were strikes and protests. In other places there were armed uprisings. By the end of the 1950s, a handful of African nations—including Morocco, Tunisia, and Ghana—had gained independence. Most of the continent would follow during the next decade.

turned them into state-run businesses. Castro also declared that America held too much control over Cuba. His government seized land owned by US companies. Relations between the two countries deteriorated, and America stopped all trade with Castro's government. Ultimately, Castro would embrace communism and turn to the Soviet Union for economic assistance. The United States would have to learn to deal with having a communist nation as a close neighbor. Many Cubans seeking a better life from under the thumb of communism fled to Florida.

The Suez Crisis

The Suez Canal was built in Egypt in the mid-1800s, when the country was still controlled by the British. The British allowed ships of all nations to use the canal, which enables easy access between Europe and Asia. In 1956, an independent Egypt seized the canal. Britain, France, and Israel feared that Egypt would close the waterway to certain nations. Already, Israeli ships were banned from using the Suez Canal. Egyptian president Gamal Abdel Nasser refused to cede control of the Suez Canal.

On October 29, 1956, as part of a secret plan between Israel, Britain, and France to capture the canal and punish Nasser, Israel launched a surprise attack against Egypt. One week later, British and French forces attacked Egypt, as well. The Egyptian army was unable to stop them. Though defeated, Nasser chose to deprive the invaders of their prize. He purposely sank forty ships inside the canal to block any other ships from using the waterway.

The rest of the world watched the Suez crisis with alarm. As with Korea, there was concern that it could grow into a world war. The United Nations ordered a halt to the fighting and sent UN peacekeepers to the canal to restore order. Within two months, control of the Suez Canal was returned to Egypt. UN workers removed the sunken ships. The canal reopened for shipping in early 1957.

Port Said, the entrance to the Suez Canal from the Mediterranean, was reduced to rubble.

Advances in Science, Technology, and Medicine

The 1950s saw remarkable advances in medicine. For the first time, doctors were able to treat many deadly diseases, including polio. Dr. John H. Gibbon Jr. performed the first successful open-heart surgery, and America launched its first satellite into orbit.

Computers Become More Widespread

When Remington Rand introduced its UNIVAC computer in 1951, people were amazed at how small it was. It was fourteen by seven by nine feet—about the size of a small bedroom! Today, this seems enormous. But it was only about one tenth of the size of earlier computers.

Throughout the 1950s, computers became smaller, faster, and more powerful machines. Many businesses and academic institutions could finally afford them. Transistors replaced vacuum tubes, making the smaller machines possible. The silicon microchip, a small wafer of silicon, was developed in 1958 to 1959. Jack Kilby at Texas Instruments placed electronic circuits onto microchips. Robert Noyce at Fairchild Semiconductor invented a way to connect microchip circuits. Continual advances in miniaturization in the decades to come would eventually lead to today's hand-held computers that have greater capabilities than the room-sized UNIVAC of the 1950s.

univac
FAC-TRONIC SYSTEM

BY *Remington Rand*
ECKERT-MAUCHLY

Remington Rand
Univac Electronic Computer

The UNIVAC was considered small for a computer.

Jack Kilby was the coinventor of the integrated circuit.

Surgical Advances

Before the 1950s, operating on the heart was nearly impossible. The heart pumps blood through the body. If the heart stopped beating during surgery, the patient would die. In 1953, an American doctor named John Gibbon solved that problem. He invented a heart-lung machine. The device pumped blood through the patient's body. It allowed doctors to stop the heart so they could operate on it. Today, open-heart surgery is common.

The first successful organ transplant took place in 1954. Dr. Joseph Murray of Boston, Massachusetts, performed the surgery. His patient needed a new kidney. Murray transplanted a kidney donated by the patient's twin brother.

Software programs were another major innovation. One of the earliest programming languages was FORTRAN, which was used for science and mathematics. Then came COBOL, or Common Business Oriented Language, which was used for business. This was the start of what is known today as the Information Age.

The Race to Space

Before 1957, humanity had never ventured into space. On October 4 of that year, the Soviet Union launched *Sputnik 1*, the world's first man-made satellite, into orbit around the earth. Many Americans reacted with shock, outrage, and fear at this demonstration of Soviet superiority in space. Secretary of Defense Charles Wilson tried to calm fears by saying *Sputnik* was nothing more than a "neat scientific trick." President Eisenhower said there was nothing to worry about "as far as security is concerned." Most Americans, of course, disagreed. The United States was involved in a nuclear arms race with the Soviet Union. It now appeared likely that America's rival would soon be able to launch nuclear missiles at the United States from space. Americans were amazed that their country could have fallen so far behind the Soviet Union in rocket technology. Suddenly, government money began to pour into space research. President Eisenhower created the National Aeronautics and Space Administration, or NASA. The new agency would manage the nation's spaceflight efforts.

When the United States successfully launched its first satellite, *Explorer 1*, into orbit on January 31, 1958, Soviet leader Nikita Khrushchev had a good laugh. He pointed out that the American satellite weighed only thirty pounds, whereas the Soviets were launching satellites that weighed more than a thousand pounds. He referred to *Explorer 1* as a "little grapefruit." But America would ultimately have the last laugh when the *Apollo* astronauts won the space race by walking on the surface of the moon a decade later.

Sputnik *was the first artificial satellite launched into space.*

Laika

One month after *Sputnik 1* was launched, the Soviets launched the larger *Sputnik 2* satellite. A dog named Laika onboard the craft became the first animal to orbit Earth. Laika means barker in Russian. A Moscow street dog, Laika was one of three dogs chosen to undergo training by Soviet scientists. The scientists chose stray dogs with the idea that they would be able to withstand extreme cold and hunger. With the other dogs as backup, Laika was launched into orbit on November 3, 1957. However, Laika was not expected to survive the full trip. She was closely monitored from Earth so that Soviet scientists could learn how animals would adapt to conditions on the craft and in space. After about five hours in flight, Laika's vital signs were undetectable. The heat and stress of the event killed her.

A Breakthrough in DNA

Scientists were also involved in work outside the space race. They were making great progress in learning how the human body works. Genes within the deoxyribonucleic acid, or DNA, in the nucleus of each of our cells carry the code for manufacturing the various proteins that allow the cells to function. Until the 1950s, very little was known about the structure of DNA and how genes function.

In the early 1950s, Rosalind Franklin used an X-ray photographic technique to determine that DNA is helical, or spiral, in form. Then, in 1953, American biologist James Watson worked with English biophysicist Francis Crick to discover that DNA is formed by two helixes wound around each other. They then found that the double helix could unwind to allow the structure to duplicate itself exactly. These discoveries would lead to breakthroughs in the study of the genetic code on which all life is based, and an understanding of which genes are responsible for certain characteristics in human beings.

Jonas Salk Defeats Polio

Epidemics of polio, often referred to as infantile paralysis, had long occurred in many parts of the world, including the United States, Europe, and Asia. A particularly severe outbreak of the disease had begun in the United States in 1942 and continued into the 1950s. In 1950 alone there were some thirty-three thousand reported cases of the disease.

Jonas Salk, an American research scientist, had begun working in 1947 to find a way to prevent the crippling disease. After several years of painstaking work in his laboratory, Salk found that by injecting a killed polio virus into a person, the body could build up an immunity to stronger forms of the virus. He developed a polio vaccine and proved it was safe by testing it on himself, his wife, and his children.

In 1954, more than 1.8 million schoolchildren were injected with the vaccine. In 1955, the vaccine was declared safe and effective in preventing polio. A serious disease had been conquered by a man of science.

Jonas Salk's vaccine protected millions of children from polio.

Conclusion

The 1950s were a time of great prosperity for many Americans, as well as a period of contrast and change. Middle-class families were doing well in the years after World War II. Millions of children were being born, and families who could afford it were fulfilling dreams of home ownership in the suburbs. Television portrayed middle-class life as an ideal. Americans huddled together to watch their favorite television stars live wonderful lives in an idealized, fictitious suburban world.

At the same time, Americans were often huddling in fear. The tense years of the Cold War, the arms race, and Senator McCarthy's hunt for communists caused people to fear a nuclear war could occur at any time. Even children, who took part in duck-and-cover drills and watched their families build fallout shelters, felt this overwhelming apprehension. Others had different fears. African Americans feared racist violence as they struggled to win the civil rights denied them for so long.

The 1950s were marked by all of these ups and downs. From the terror caused by *Sputnik* to the birth of rock 'n' roll, from the war in Korea to the poodle skirt, the 1950s were truly a unique and amazing decade.

By the last months of 1959, Washington was abuzz with rumors. Many news reporters and political insiders believed that a young US Senator from Massachusetts was planning to run for president in 1960. They were right. On January 2, 1960—the second day of the new decade—John F. Kennedy announced his candidacy. In July, he received the Democratic Party's nomination. In November, Kennedy won the election against Republican Richard Nixon.

America's space program symbolized a new era that focused on the future.

Kennedy was the first president born in the twentieth century. At forty-three, he was also the youngest man elected to the nation's highest office. In his first speech as president, Kennedy told the country, "The torch has been passed to a new generation of Americans." Kennedy said that the United States would meet all the challenges presented by its enemies, especially the Soviet Union. But he also said that ways had to be found to lessen the chances of a nuclear war. He asked Americans to work for the good of their country, and he called on people everywhere to work for human freedom. With his youth, his energy, and his bold words, Kennedy inspired many people. He created a sense of optimism about the future.

Some great achievements would, in fact, occur during the 1960s. The civil rights movement would succeed in getting rid of laws that had made African Americans second-class citizens. Astronauts would walk on the moon and return safely to earth. Yet the 1960s would also be a time of conflict and turmoil—a situation exemplified by the assassination of President John F. Kennedy less than three years after he took office.

Timeline

1950 Christian Dior's New Look is the height of fashion. Ben Hogan wins the US Open golf tournament. Joseph McCarthy announces that he has a list of communists working in the State Department, which begins the McCarthy Red Scare. Ethel and Julius Rosenberg are arrested for espionage. North Korea invades South Korea, which begins the Korean War.

1951 J. D. Salinger publishes *The Catcher in the Rye*. The Rosenbergs are convicted of espionage. President Harry Truman fires General Douglas MacArthur. UNIVAC computer is introduced.

1952 Rocky Marciano first wins world heavyweight title. Dwight D. Eisenhower is elected president on the Republican ticket.

1953 The movies *War of the Worlds*, *House of Wax*, and *It Came from Outer Space* are released. Marilyn Monroe stars in *Gentlemen Prefer Blondes* and *How to Marry a Millionaire*. Ben Hogan becomes Associated Press Male Athlete of the Year. The Rosenbergs die in the electric

chair. Armistice is signed in the Korean War. The Eisenhower administration establishes Department of Health, Education, and Welfare. Soviet leader Joseph Stalin dies. Dr. John Gibbon Jr. performs the first successful open-heart surgery. Scientists James Watson and Francis Crick discover the structure and function of DNA.

1954 Marlon Brando stars in *The Wild One. Creature from the Black Lagoon* is released. The Army-McCarthy hearings take place with the help of McCarthy aide Roy Cohn. The US Supreme Court hands down its *Brown v. Board of Education* decision.

1955 *Rebel Without a Cause* opens in theaters. *The Blackboard Jungle* draws attention to gang-related violence in New York City. Brooklyn Dodgers defeat the New York Yankees in the World Series. Rosa Parks inspires African American leaders, including Martin Luther King Jr., to start the Montgomery Bus Boycott. Jonas Salk's polio vaccine is declared safe and effective.

1956 Congress passes the National Defense Highway Act to build more highways for defense and recreational driving. The film *Invasion of the Body Snatchers* becomes a hit. *The Ten Commandments* opens in theaters. Rocky Marciano retires from professional boxing. Dwight Eisenhower is reelected president. The US Supreme Court declares bus segregation laws in Montgomery, Alabama, unconstitutional. Nikita Khrushchev becomes leader of Soviet Union. Hungary attempts to revolt against Soviet control.

1957 Jack Kerouac publishes *On the Road*. Brooklyn Dodgers move at the end of the baseball season to become the Los Angeles Dodgers. Althea Gibson becomes the first black person to win Wimbledon and US Open singles tennis titles. Senator Joseph McCarthy dies. The first civil rights act since Reconstruction is passed. President Eisenhower sends troops to help integrate Little Rock's Central High School. The Soviet Union launches *Sputnik 1*.

1958 Althea Gibson, for the second consecutive year, wins Wimbledon and US Open singles titles. The United States launches *Explorer 1*. The hula hoop is introduced.

1959 The film *Ben-Hur* opens in theaters. Marilyn Monroe appears in *Some Like It Hot*. Fidel Castro succeeds in ousting Cuban dictator Fulgencio Batista and becomes the dictator of Cuba.

Glossary

abstract expressionist—Art movement occurring after World War II that put American—specifically New York—painting at the forefront of the art world.

beatnik—Member of the 1950s subculture associated with the beat generation.

bracero—Mexican laborer performing seasonal work in America.

canal—A man-made waterway that allows ships to shorten their journey.

colony—A territory that is controlled by a distant nation.

communism—A type of political and economic system in which all citizens are supposed to share work and property equally.

crisis—An unstable situation; an emergency.

espionage—Spying.

orbit—The path of an object as it revolves around a planet or other mass.

polio— Short for poliomyelitis, a highly contagious disease that at its worst can lead to paralysis and even death.

population—The total number of people living in an area.

rapt—Fascinated or enthralled.

revolution—Sweeping change that leads to the overthrow of a government.

satellite—An orbiting object in space.

segregation—The practice of keeping people separate based on race or other differences.

superpower—An extremely powerful country, especially one that leads other countries.

transplant—The act of taking an organ from one body and putting it into another.

transportation—The business of moving people or goods.

truce—An agreement to stop fighting; a cease-fire.

Further Reading

Books

Boucher, Diane. *The 1950s American Home*. Oxford, England: Shire, 2013.

Halberstam, David. *The Fifties*. New York: Villard Books, 1993.

Immel, Myra (ed.). *Cuban Revolution*. Detroit: Greenhaven Press, 2013.

Immel, Myra (ed.). *The McCarthy Era*. Detroit: Greenhaven Press, 2011.

McNeese, Tim. *The Cold War and Postwar America*. New York: Chelsea House, 2010.

Mieczkowski, Yanek. *Eisenhower's Sputnik Moment*. Ithaca, N.Y.: Cornell University Press, 2013.

Web Sites

coldwar.org/
Cold War Museum Web site, which also includes online exhibits.

koreanwar.org/
The Korean War Project is a resource for veterans, their families, and historians.

whitehouse.gov/history/presidents/de34.html
The White House's official fact page for President Dwight D. Eisenhower.

fiftiesweb.com/
The Fifties Index focuses on 1950s popular culture.

Movies

Gentlemen Prefer Blondes. Directed by Howard Hawks. Los Angeles, Calif.: 20th Century Fox, 1953.

Marilyn Monroe stars in this big-budget musical.

Good Night and Good Luck. Directed by George Clooney. Dallas, Tex.: 2929 Entertainment, 2005.

Dramatizes journalist Edward R. Murrow's clash with Senator Joseph McCarthy.

Index

31901059212375